AN EYELASH FOR SAND

Selected Poems by Michael Kwong

An Eyelash For Sand

Cover art and drawings of instruments were created during free jazz performances in New York. Abstract paintings and portraits were made using acrylics, watercolor, wood, and canvas.

Printed in the United States of America
First Printing, 2024

ISBN 979-8-9915220-0-7

www.kwongart.com

TABLE OF CONTENTS

CYLINDER

Gripped with curved fingers
Bold beneath the challenge of elevation
Lies upon
My intoxicating
Science of reverie

Molten gold
Prying its way
From helpless
Gravity unchallenged beings
I touch every corner

Divide
And subdivide again
Parceled to your feet
I ride the course of the sun's rotation
Glazing over my rim
Trapping in stance

My teeth will not contrive you
My polish invites you
To balance on the ways of the world below deck

THE FLOWER CITY

I.
The flower city opened its wings, pouring the lifeblood of the artist
From shell as body
To a pane of volume and metrics

Each flask, obsolete only to the seeing eye
Captured the moments of undulation
Where lapses, denounced into constriction, formed a path

With golden steps uncharted
The infinitesimal power of essence unlatched anatomy
Curving around a tongue that touches all

II.
Miracles unfolding
A gallery where lapses once lay to rest
The flower city spread its tones upon metal, blending the hardwood floor

Artists in release
Floating their tobacco to the smokestacks above
Light curved matches on opaque tinder
Silent to the residue of destruction in their wake

SALVATION

His stern brow
Hastening the dark beats
Pulled you under
The Invasion

A flagstone of sores
Maritime and hardened
Repaid its salt

Spinning wide
Lifting sickness to a rise
Pressing enunciation
The envelopes churned
Tongue brimming
With the glass rim of a nation

The metal silos
Enigmatic as poison dreams
Deafening
Cacophonous together
Swallowed

Emergent arms
Bringing screams to pace
Your sentence undeniable
Fire ripped from air
Salivating your time

Bending redemption forward
He walks the tiles of agony
Hard light distilled
Slouching without remorse

PRINCESS

Sweet candy calamity
Sidestep
Forward gaze
Chromatic violation, stretching the periphery of hair and nails

Her ears turned inward
Vanity on a path of struggling stone
She reached beyond the moors, bending decadence to her will

A palanquin in pale
Infallible
Undeniable
Turning waists like pop-up tops
Shining skin in the glass jars of augury

Enticed she waited
With glitter of translucent daze
Sparkles deadened to a thud
The backdrops folding backwards
The splinter of metallic hinge
How she must have felt, such yellow eyes upon her

Now powder failing
Clocks inverting
Pulse racing toward satin resurrection
Sweat is ailing
Conscience falling
Wounds unmending
Tethered and tied
Forward

Shallow
Still stepped the moon
Bringing green gashes to tyrannize our dark medallion's purest line

Toes first
Ankles first
Hips inverted
Triumph over the tailwind of our animals in robe

Undaunted

Our ocean released its eyes
Silence unspoken
Sand insistent
She churned exaltation below

The water nodded
The jesters pounced to their graves
And through endless dissipation
She found currents to reclaim her peace

AN EYELASH FOR SAND

Ankles for angels
Flesh on the facts of neutrality
You signed a post as pioneer
So I spat blood through a hexagram of ages, marking hallowed ground

A silhouette seven layers deep
Undusted
Ripping sheen from shelter protests and scoured condominiums

The iris of change
Humming goodnight moon to the left side of burnt bodies
Broke the devil, but failed to mention a second course

Now you stand in nightshade
Wonder fading through the confines of open arms
Progress welded to fate, like mirrors on the axis of a spade
Unbecoming

A kiss from crown to solemnity, bounces forward
Waiting
Hands forever untied

GLASS SPHERES

The will
The will to lift your arm
To unwind your fingers against the night's aching palette
Syphoning the colors of under-painted remorse

As a child, you captured only the smallest doses of memory
Calling the vials to your side
Recounting the mystery of glass spheres

Resting by the window that concedes to the deck
You sought only truth, nothing more
Signing over your deepest regrets

Burying the seeds to match them
You entered the exercise with quietest of minds
Tracing in the most common of tongues

Seeds turned
A basin of resurgence
        Moments of struggle
Regret forms a canopy
Sewing together lost desires
Lost spaces better left untouched

The sunlight, leaking from the sutures above
Strike the absence of definition

And what could have been more exacting?
Truth in its palest form
Resting in your brilliant collage

SELFISH

Blue is more passionate than the pavilion of time
Her black hair and curved fingers
Weigh in

A simple lash of lace and ivy
Crescent the fall from memory to savage
Moans of ambition and foresight
Break through clouds
Constant
Unabated flashes of rosemary on lust

Chasing the lines between ages and beauty
She focused on broken
I found her in rhyme
Aching
Motion
Forward shredding creases of tongue
Toes blistering in the neon lights of Brooklyn filth
We could have lapsed forever

The common cause of red on vinyl
She rested
Under
Thinnest of glaze, wrecked in perception

Touching
Through the length of silence she dropped
Crashing like sand on a circlet of jade

Standing alone
Selfish
We watched
The parting of conscience from the ghosts that repelled her tongue

INSPIRATION AS HAUNTING

Weighed down by coarseness of light
The libertine spoke softly from his wooden chair

Wrists lashed to the radiators
He unleashed his echo
A dark wave, breaking windowpanes and bellowing hallways

His erratic pleasures
Melded her silence to walls recognizable
Sturdy
Coated in white with red of blood

His conscience
Drove the neon lights to the scene of broken bottles
The philistine's laugh, stretching on the concrete below

Insubstantial
She stood in defiance of a world she could not claim
Pulling at her tone like salt breaking through a cloth

Fraught
Our magnum opus
Our dark catalyst of egress
Redirected his gaze towards her polished eyes

The artist, between them, drawing from each in kind
Poured his vanity beneath shades of paper
Haunting with the promise of colonial power

As wooden floorboards
Settled the final motion of the clock's broken tongue
The libertine wretched, switched with the scent of England beneath his skin

With every movement
Our Geist laid bare her intent
Sweeping with the red taint of open arms

Wrists unfolding
She broke her audience upon the stage of reckoning
Eyes pinned in their struggle
Shuttering, begging to revere her undeniable form

ALLOPATHY

Several layers of infinite seas
Potentized
Render the star of cosmetic glee
The physician stared
Perennial conscience lifting into tar and lime

Now your awaited hope
Porcelain rage filtered onto a tarp of unbreakable form

Cheeks pressed to a doorknob
Wisdom
A master of sand preaches four stories to the right

Broken but faded
You emerge, ready to repress again

SEVERANCE

The mirrors of shame, sanitized her act of forgiveness
When everywhere
And everyone
Were bracing through windows

Her bitter self followed the long line
Breaking hips on an analogy of song
Encircling grace in concrete of malice

Shining from right angles
The mirrors battered her darkest impulse
Hollowing language
Pulling utterance from the depth of her tongue

The primacy of her sex split
Each tone dropping to its roots
Pacing the floorboards
Pushing callous beneath splinters

A sharp turn
Folds in reflection
The sidelines around her beckon for redemption

String stretches
Color and tether formed
Windows kiss at their distance
The angst of periphery, like contrast burnt sideways

The mirrors
Flooded with dreams of yellow creases
Sailed her ships
Prostituting her beauty from eyebrow to ether skies

Singing the common song
She cracked with smoke
Opened with vanilla, then dried to a crisp
Seeing only formation, her skin pried itself of lines and lingering
Chaos swallowed whole

Unforetold, she trailed your demise
Nails apparent but softened to a touch

Reaching and gripping, pulling on your lungs
Heart
Science
And mind

A gentle pause
Her hair lashes the last shard of perception
Knees falling forward
She parts the film, interjecting her smile

A COMPOSITION IN RED

At autumn's edge
I brought blood and rage to the builders' hearts
Decomposed, but ready at separation

Tainted by silver
I balanced on a flask of metaphor by design
Refuting soil and gods
Yet somehow
The seeds of romantic tracing

Filter my breath
Pulse of an untouched secret
Undermine space
Surrendering to a table where labor and idols sought harmony

An indentation of wrists
Bending rightward over a breach of sand
Bring solemn to the shape of hearts
Combing its final announcement
Compounding effort under fire and smoke

With desire extracted
Played upon
I meddled into madness
Anointing pauper
Running deeper towards the sun's
Inevitable titration

An acolyte of reunion
A burnt allocation
Walking romance from shape to bow
Under siege and underperformed
I strove beyond constraint
Gesturing to a beacon of hair upon smiles

Elbows raising
Eager towards the sound of fresh angles
I raptured into collusion
A soft intervention
To bring purpose to the builders' hearts

ELIZABETH

Serum sound
I pulled from the bay the quiet space between your lips
Ribbons of love and lust turning downward

The shades of reflection, almost jealous
Exhale
Returning to form

OUR WICKED LADY

The constellation of memory
Flowing thick in white
Enveloping the pyramids
Left her side

Sadly
A product of mind produced such revolt
Leaving him gasping
Unrelenting
As she secured the flow of her time

Light is not a disgrace when you wear dark glasses
It only penetrates further
Succulent to the shadows of art
Rocking in tune to a dry alibi

Patiently she asked
What more could be expected from a shell of a man?
Plastering his shadow to the wall
Enviable, to the envied
A poster boy of pain?

Memory in action was only ever two things at once
Yet tonight it flowed in its own accordance
Never again to be constrained

QUOTATION

Brussels
Of shit and cigarette smoke
Of filth of artists
Nihilists
On their backs
Casting truces to steeples of black sky

I'm burning your regimentation
Moving across cobbled stone
Wrecking your dreams with this nicotine corpse
Buried in contradiction

And now for the runaway
A forehead filled with plastered rose
Pulsing its irritation
On silken blots of borrowed tar

Down the avenue
A music man winds his chariot box
Binding sadness to time and coffer to coin

And what a ridiculous outcome
This callous flag of black and gold
Elevating the heat of the jungle
Almost has me standing straight

Breaking the avenue's decline
A mercurial palace sits wide against the city's poison dreams
Martyring another culture for a breath of fresh air

But I won't follow foundation
Inhale the vapors
Or bury the orthodox

I'd rather stretch recklessly into the night
Spitting rain into the gutter
Prying my eyelids
Until my retinas burn sharply across the sky

ELLE

Resolve left untouched
the essence of your departure from the sick
Complicated by time
Complicated by grace
Now pushing paper sand into the mouths of compliant moths, halfway returned
Dissolution of rotting wood, mind breaking over a thimble from stem to crown

Closer Now
Cracks more apparent
Mildew and porches left in abandon
Magnetized forth.   Reset into stone
Sinking forward.   Downward
Her purple hair creases the skin of your lips

The fire of your time rakes an internal screech
Wishing you had forsaken her kindness
Cleanliness
Latch and fold

Now a body inverted, you pay penance to a sky which does not judge you
But compels a single shoulder to the earth

LITIGATION

The frame
Pushed by glutton
Traced its form to his tongue

Wanton
Our drunken triumph staggered in his way

Oh great storm of unshallow places
Oh great tears of refute
Resting elbows upon thy table
Sorting pristine marbles of hardship

The challenge of undue restraint
Setting the premier moment
Boosted an inhale

Culling with an exhale
He returned to them laughter
Our king of kings
The butterfat rolling

Following a terrifying recoil
He found his gelatin
Sealing the boundaries

Suit pressed with hands
Shoulders falling
He pried the residue from his fingernails
Propping up the last dye of an uncanny smile

Satisfied
          He receded
Swatting over the remains of that precious time

THE LITTLE

I.
I've waited for you too
Tired of death
On solid concrete

Were the lampposts shaking?
The wind blanching your hair
Snow upon blond
Red lips in contrast?

Were the gaps in time
Receded spaces
Where new twine was shorn
Recollected
And cast afar?

II.
In the cold light of sun
Ready for devotion
Traced to the hilt of flesh
I called to you

Who returned peace
A collage of threads
Painted in desire